Creative Writing in the Classroom

Carol Staudacher

PITMAN LEARNING, INC.
Belmont, California

ISBN-0-8224-1680-8

Library of Congress Catalog Card Number: 68-55314

Printed in the United States of America.

Contents

1 *Setting the Creative Climate*

You, as a teacher, cannot do any creative thinking for a child and you certainly cannot *carry through* the creative process for him. However, you do have an extremely important part to play in the child's creative production. You provide the motivation and the encouragement, and you set the creative climate.

To begin with, you must develop an atmosphere that will break down the reservations and inhibitions that block the child's creative tendencies. Establishing a good "talking" relationship with children is the first step, keeping in mind the fact that all conversation need not be motivated by specific educational goals or the learning of facts. Conversation, like anything else, can be creative—and in many instances it is more creative than the written word since speaking comes easier and more naturally than writing. It is in everyday speech that an alert teacher will see signs of creativity.

Very small children will often talk in delightful prose without even realizing it. For example, a child of three or four when hearing the rain pound on the roof might say, "A big man goes boom-boom on our house." When referring to a house of shingles a small child may identify it by saying, "They live in the wrinkled house." Upon hearing a baby using one-syllable sounds, a six-year-old said, "He scribbles when he talks."

Author Nelson Algren has said, "The poetry comes from the people who don't read poems," meaning that the inarticulate often have their own innate gift for saying poetic things. So it is with children, also.

As children get older they learn the rules imposed upon them by maturity. They become self-conscious about their speech for fear of making mistakes or sounding babyish. It is up to the teacher to free the inborn urge that children have to express themselves poetically. Stimulating the child's thinking along non-academic lines leads him to discover and voice thoughts he never realized he had. He can use these thoughts as a basis for his writing when he begins it. Thus, in conversation with children, incidental talk of the weather, spring signs, how a storm makes you feel, how certain music makes you feel, what a picture makes you think about, can all take on a creative touch.

In the pages to follow I will suggest specific methods and materials for you to use before various assignments in order to enrich the creative climate of your classroom.

Fundamental Rules

There are certain fundamental rules to follow before each creative writing assignment. These can be applied to the classroom no matter what type of creative writing you are experimenting with. First, the children have to be freed of their grammar worries if they are to be able to let their creativeness work. When they are hampered by trying to remember whether to use "Susan and I" or "Susan and me," they are delaying their original thoughts and forcing them to come second to the rules of grammar. They should not have to think about whether to use a semicolon or a comma or whether or not to start a new paragraph. *If a child's creative thoughts have to be sidetracked, he may lose a very original idea.* This very thing is frustrating to an adult when he is writing, but it is even more frustrating to a child who is conscious of having his errors singled out and marked.

Second, children will automatically worry about spelling. I have always emphasized the "special spelling rule" in regard to any creative writing children do. I tell the children at the beginning, "When you write creatively I do not expect you to worry about your spelling. You may spell the word the way it sounds and correct it later. The main thing to remember is to get your thoughts down on paper as well as you can and to use your own original ideas."

If a child knows that he will have an opportunity later to correct errors and that his paper will not be strictly graded on mechanics, he will be relieved of a few of his doubts about being imaginative. The ideal method of correcting creative writing is to go over each paper individually with the young author and discuss, in order of importance, the idea, the method used to convey the idea, and the mechanical errors.

Sometimes this ideal method is not possible. As an alternative, a teacher with a large group could read over what the children have written for one specific assignment. Then he could compile a few notes on the most common mistakes and discuss them with the class. It is quite possible to give constructive criticism about the errors without mentioning the pupils' names or stories. It is good for the child to know in advance that this is going to happen so that he will know how his errors will be handled. Explaining it to your group beforehand will make them more willing and happy to create. This should take care of their "mechanical worries."

At all times the teacher must remember to give more emphasis, attention, and praise to the creative ideas expressed by the child than to grammatical or technical difficulties in the child's writing.

This may sound like putting the cart before the horse to some teachers, but it really is not. It is definitely one of the most important things to keep in mind if you are going to stimulate a classroom of children to write creatively.

The Child's Writing

You will find that a child's ability in his regular academic subjects has little to do with how creative he can be. Many children who are not good readers, who lack enthusiasm for school, who are withdrawn or even hostile can excel in creative writing. Furthermore, many of the children who do well in other subjects find creative writing a new outlet or an interesting challenge. Once creative writing is properly motivated almost all children enjoy it. Only very few children do not. They will come to class with ideas of their own about something they want to write, or some of them will begin writing at home and bring what they have created to school to show to you.

I have found that the strongest incentive for elementary children when they begin trying to write creatively is to hear other children's writing read to them. For this reason I have included many samples of children's work along with specific creative writing lessons. In the children's writing presented in this book I have occasionally corrected spelling and punctuation to make it more easily readable. However, word usage, paragraphs, methods, and so on, have all been left intact. In most cases no corrections at all were made. All the stories, poems, and other writings are products of an average class. I have selected a cross section of writing that shows creativity at all levels. It is here for you to use as an incentive for your own class. Children respond more quickly to hearing something written by someone at their own age and grade level than they do to hearing an adult's creative work read.

2 Description

Description is an integral part of creative writing. Because the children will be using it in their poetry and short stories, it is a good place for us to begin. Description is easy for children to understand and once they have tried it, they can quickly see some results of their creative efforts.

First, as a group, discuss what description is. It tells something. It gives the reader a "mind picture" of an object, person, place, or feeling. It helps the reader visualize, smell, taste, touch, or hear something.

To begin with, have the children bring in and share magazine advertisements, for they are easy to obtain and are almost totally descriptive. The pupils can discuss the effectiveness of each description. Was the ad interesting? Did it do a good job of describing something? The children may like to select unusual adjectives that they thought helped the description. They may substitute adjectives of their own and see how they sound. In lower grades this would be done on a smaller scale, of course, and the use of the word *adjective* would not be necessary at all.

As a next step the children could select descriptions from stories they have read, and then read them aloud to the class to test the effectiveness of each description. Asking them, "Could you see it? Could you hear it? Could you smell it . . . taste it?" Someone in the class could draw a picture of the thing being described the way he saw it and the description could be pinned up along with the picture. In this way the children will realize that they can create pictures in the minds of other people by the use of their own words.

As a beginning oral lesson in description you can make up hypothetical situations and let the children describe them aloud so that it is a group experience. They will realize then how easy description is to express. For example, you could say, "I have my eyes closed and am entering a store where chocolate candy is made and sold. What do I smell? How can you describe it?" Some typical reactions might be, "It smelled warm and sweet." "It made your stomach growl and your mouth water." Or you could say, "I have been knocked down by a huge, cold wave and am getting up. How do I feel? What do I taste?" Then responses will come about the taste of the water, the coldness, the salt stinging the eyes, feet sinking in the sand as the ocean rushes back out, and so on. Provoking oral description is fun for the teacher and the children love it. At the same time, without being aware of it, they are establishing a background for an essential part of writing.

After experimenting with oral description a few times, have each of the children select one object, person, or place that he likes or dislikes very much. Most children will select one almost immediately. If anyone has trouble doing this you could suggest that they describe something that they have seen and will never forget. Stress that it should be just *one* object or thing.

A good gimmick for keeping their enthusiasm during this first writing experience is to give them a small piece of paper to write on so that they will not feel that a lot is expected of them. They will not be overwhelmed by a large, blank space to fill. Give them a few minutes to write some sentences describing their object, person, or whatever they have chosen. Then collect the descriptions and read them back to the class immediately, giving as much praise as possible to each one, carefully pointing out the good points you find in each description. If some children ask to have theirs left unread just hold them at the bottom of the pile. Eventually their reluctance to share their creativity will be forgotten.

The key to getting children to produce creatively is to make them believe in what they are doing and be proud of it. This is done by showing enthusiasm for original ideas, commenting favorably on them and encouraging their growth. Confidence in their ability to write creatively should be fostered all along the creative road, but it is most important in the beginning so that the children sense your sincerity and therefore can give more of *their* sincerity to their creative work without being self-conscious.

Following are some examples of descriptions written by elementary children the first time they were introduced to description by this method.

As I ate the butter-drenched popcorn it melted in my mouth with the most tender, juicy and delicious flavor. The curved ends crunched in my watery mouth. They looked as if they were shined with polish because of the rich butter and salt they had been soaked in.

(Sixth grade student)

The baby's skin felt as soft and smooth as skin could get. Her eyes shone like the sun and her hair was finer than the finest thread.

(Third grade student)

The battered, dusty, old model T sits in the garage on the grass. It used to be a beautiful car that not many people had but now it stays in the dirty garage waiting to see if anyone will notice it again.

(Fifth grade student)

The table was old and worn. It lay in the cellar all year until it was put in the den to make more room in the cellar. The dirty, ugly, worn table was fixed up so it looked like it was still living. Then we sat down to eat. The table was now part of the family.

(Fifth grade student)

Sharing descriptions such as these will encourage the children to continue trying to write descriptively and improve their ability. They are a great audience for each other and will appreciate a classmate's effort just as quickly as the teacher will.

Later, after they have written description once in the above manner they can try it again to see how many senses they can involve. Before the second lesson let the class select one thing to describe. Then ask them to make the description so clear to the reader that it appeals to as many of the five senses (touch, taste, hearing, smell, sight) as possible. It would be unfair to insist that all of them involve all five senses in their description but some may want to try it as an extra challenge.

Here are a few simple descriptions I have used with fourth, fifth, and sixth graders as examples of descriptions that create a definite mood or develop a definite mental image.

The wet vines cling to the side of the huge wall, their moisture dripping down between the cracks in the bricks. Small, glistening bugs wander about on the flat, green leaves and hide themselves.

The forgotten island stood in the middle of the sea that lay like glass without a shimmer. One tree on the island was taller than all the rest. It stretched its top up to the brightest blue in the sky and stayed there lonely and looking down.

That night everything was completely still except for one very sharp, clear sound. It was the constant shrill of a cricket calling to nobody, calling to nobody again and again with its tiny, metal-like voice echoing in the blackness.

The water was cool and frothy as she plunged into the breakers. It swirled and swished its way around her, plastering her dark hair slickly against her head and shoulders.

Sounds of a busy gaiety filled the air. Carnival men beckoned in loud, harsh voices, "Step right up here . . . Step right up here . . . This way folks . . . Just a quarter!" Swishing skirts and laughter whirled by on the Merry-Go-Round, and throughout the night a thousand happy voices called to one another.

These descriptions could be used as the basis for a discussion on how a description actually sets a mood, how it makes the reader feel a certain way. The children can tell what they felt after each one. You might ask them to compare the third and fifth descriptions. In the fifth there is a busyness, a feeling of action and of noise. The third one definitely established a quiet mood. The children may then like to try writing a description that sets a definite mood, by selecting the mood beforehand and writing to that end.

Overworking description before they have had other writing experiences can diminish the children's enthusiasm; so after about three tries at it, you should go on to another form of writing, keeping in mind that you have laid the groundwork for much of their future poetry and story writing.

3 *Writing Stories*

There are many ways to stimulate story writing. Among them are the use of pictures, titles, unfinished stories, folk tales, and storybook characters. In this chapter each of these ways of encouraging children to write stories will be discussed.

The Use of Pictures

One of the most common ways to stimulate primary grade children is with pictures. Many teachers who use this method are not particularly pleased with the results because the stories they get from their children are too much alike. The stories do not show inventiveness. The problem here is usually that the teacher is not careful about the type of picture he chooses. He may select a picture for the children to write about which *tells* the story in itself. A picture of a tiger leaping out of a jungle onto a hunter is going to produce stories about a hunter being attacked by a tiger. A picture of a happy family standing around a brand new car is going to produce stories about a happy family getting a brand new car. In cases such as these the child will merely be recording automatically what he sees in the picture.

The pictures that are most effective are the ones that leave quite a lot to the imagination. They show something to arouse interest, to stimulate the child's mind, to put his imagination to work, but do not completely tell their own story. A second grade boy who had been shown a picture of a round-eyed boy sitting in tall, yellow grass with a sleek cat in his arms, wrote the following story:

> Once upon a time there was a little boy and he had a cat. He liked the cat but the cat did not like him. One day the cat ran away. The boy could not find him. The boy started to weep. He went out to find him. He hid behind the straw. A little while later he saw the cat. Then he jumped out of the straw and caught the cat. They lived happily ever after.

Using pictures of people with expressions on their faces of awe, amazement, or surprise can stimulate creativity after the teacher asks, "Could you write a story to tell what happened to this person to make him look this way?" Or, "This person seems to be watching something. What do you think he is watching and why?"

For older children, selecting pictures of people with a lot of character in their faces is a good exercise. A wrinkled old woman, a very young child, round-eyed and laughing, a hippie, old men with walking canes, all make interesting subjects for study. You can ask the class to write a short biography of the individual they find most interesting in the pictures you have shown them.

After the children have used your pictures once or twice they may want to find their own picture of a "character" and bring it in to write about.

The following story was written by a fifth grade girl after looking at a picture of an old man.

The Black and White Zebra

Once there lived a little man who lived on an unknown land. He always wanted someone to talk to. He was a lonely little man. He was about four and a half feet tall.

One day he was walking when it started to rain. It was a funny rain because it rained chocolate. Next it rained vanilla. It rained and rained. It never stopped raining.

The little man was terrified to see it rain. He did not waste it. Instead he mixed the colors together and it came out striped. Then he made a little wooden animal. He took the white and poured it over the animal, then the black.

Before long the sky turned dark and cold. The little wooden animal turned alive at night. The little man was so excited and now with his little zebra walked happily off.

The Use of Titles

The use of titles to stimulate story writing is helpful to children who lack an idea to get them started, but do not lack imagination. Most children will fit into this category if they have not had much experience in writing. In this kind of creative writing lesson you can write several provocative titles on the board. Again, as in the use of pictures, *do not use titles that tell a story, but ones that suggest*. These titles can be your own inventions. For example, the type I have used to promote ideas but still give leeway for creativity are *The Runaway Chevrolet*, *Fun on Mars*, *The Man with the Golden Nose*, *The Clock That Wouldn't Chime*, *The Mystery of the Constant Sound*, *The Teeny Tiny Man*. The four following stories are products of this technique.

The Teeny Tiny Man

Once upon a time there lived a teeny tiny man. Because he was so tiny he could go in and out of things that we could not. His name was Teeny because he was so tiny. So one day he made his home in an old, old mouse hole. As the years went by he grew old and the owner of the home that his home was in bought a cat and the cat thought that Teeny was a mouse so like all cats when Teeny went to get some food the cat would chase Teeny. The cat was getting to be a problem. So he had to get rid of the cat. All one night Teeny was awake figuring out a plan. Then about 2:30 Teeny thought of an idea. In the morning Teeny sneaked out of the house and went to the toy store and got some toy mice. The next day Teeny wound the toy mice up and let them go. The cat was so busy catching the mice that he did not notice Teeny so Teeny could get all the food he wanted whenever he wanted and he would use the mice.

(Third grade boy)

The Clock That Wouldn't Chime

Once there were little white mice that lived under an old grandpappa clock. The mice seemed to live happily *except* when the clock was about to chime. One day one of the mice had an idea and said, "Why don't we stop the chimer?" "That's a good idea. Why don't we?" And so they did.

But every time the clock was about to chime it burped and blew up a little more. One day when all the mice were relaxing they heard a boom, crash, bang and from that day on the mice haven't been seen again but if you look hard you may even find a piece of old grandpappa clock.

(Fourth grade girl)

The Clock That Wouldn't Chime

In a faraway land called Clock Land lived a family of three. Papa Joe, Mama Hoe and Sister Moe. They were a very happy family and Papa Joe loved his work. Papa's work was making clocks, all kinds of clocks.

Papa Joe and the family had one clock they treasured dearly. It was a huge grandfather clock made of solid gold. Everyone who came into

Papa Joe's shop offered a very high price for the clock but Papa Joe just wouldn't sell it.

One day a very strange thing happened to the grandfather clock. It was one o'clock in the afternoon and the clock chimed, 1, 2, 3, 4, 5, 6, 7, 8, 9, 10, 11, 12, 13 times. Papa Joe was furious because everyone knew the clock was broken. For that matter, it never chimed again.

Papa took it to the best clock fixit shop but no one, but no one could find out what was the matter with the clock.

So from this day on if you went to Clock Land you would still hear Papa Joe, Mama Hoe and Sister Moe pleading with the clock to chime.

(Which is a pretty silly thing to do because clocks can't hear.)

(Fifth grade girl)

The Runaway Chevrolet

Once there was a '60 Chevrolet who was getting tired of going about his usual business. So he decided that very day he was going to run away. He decided that he would leave early the next morning when the family wasn't awake.

Early the next morning he sent the motor upstairs to get the keys. Then he told the steering wheel to drive and soon they were on their way. They went down Main Street so fast that when they got to the police station they had a little trouble slowing down. When the people were outside ladies screamed, babies cried, children chased the Chevrolet until he was quite worn out.

The steering wheel was turning a corner but wasn't paying any attention to his driving and "Crash!" They crashed into another car. It was a taxi and in it was the man that owned the Chevrolet. He sent the Chevrolet to the car hospital and he had an emergency operation. The Chevrolet ended up with four broken tires, a dead motor, a broken steering wheel and a few other things. But after that day the Chevrolet never ran away again. For home's the best place for cars like him.

(Sixth grade girl)

The Unfinished Story

If you find a group of children in your class who just cannot seem to get started on their own, you may tell them the first part of a story and let them write the ending. Choose a story beginning that leaves the listener "up in the air" or with a problem to solve. The following is the first part of a story that has proved successful as a story-writing stimulant to children in the fourth, fifth, and sixth grades.

Chinatown Home

Johnny Wong walked down the street of the big city with his hands in his pockets and a frown on his face. He had a big problem and he didn't know what to do about it.

Johnny walked faster and was soon in the middle of Chinatown. The policeman was standing on the corner. The red and yellow Chinese bank was shining in the sun. The ducks and chickens were ready to be sold in the small, filled Chinese shops. Everything was fine. Everybody was happy. Everyone but Johnny.

Johnny closed his eyes and rested his back against the corner of Mr. Wing's store. His teacher had said at school, "We have a paper to write. The paper will be about your pet. Tell about how you take care of your pet and about the games you play with it."

Johnny didn't want to write a paper about his pet because last Saturday his dog Chow had run away and every time he thought about it he wanted to cry. Chow had been such a good dog, and Johnny loved him so much. Why had he run away?

Johnny didn't know what to do. Tomorrow he had to give his teacher a paper about his pet, but he was too sad to write it.

He saw his mother going up the stairs to their apartment. She was pulling her shopping cart behind her. She stopped and waited for him to come inside with her. Instead, Johnny turned the other way and ran down the street. He didn't want to go home yet.

A story such as *Chinatown Home* sets a particular scene for the children and poses a problem for them to think about. They are free to bring the story to a conclusion in their own way. It is amazing how many different ways one story such as this can be ended.

For children in the primary grades a story similar to the one following is a good starter.

The Three Runaway Elephants

The circus audience cheered as the three baby elephants, Joe, John, and Jake, stood on their little round, red boxes and held their two front feet in the air. Boys and girls laughed and everyone clapped when the three little elephants performed.

But the elephants were not as happy as the circus audience. In fact they were very sad because they had to stay in the circus and entertain people. They wanted to go out and have some adventure themselves.

"I have a plan," said Jake when the show was over. "Let's go have some fun. Let's run away."

"Run away!" cried Joe and John. "We'd never get away from here."

"Oh, just let me show you," said Jake who was always smarter than the others. "I'll lead you away and they will never catch us. We'll never have to go back to the circus."

So in the middle of the night when everything was very dark and quiet, Jake made sure the trainer was asleep. Then he woke up Joe and John. "Get up! It's time to go!" he whispered.

After you have read the unfinished story to your class don't allow more than a minute or two to pass before they have their paper to finish the story. If too much time is used in discussion between the reading of the story and the finishing of the story some of the children may forget their ideas or lose the mood of the story.

Folk Tales

In the intermediate and upper grades it is especially fun to use and listen to folk tales. You can tell the children that folk tales are stories that come from early times. Sometimes they are about imaginary heroes or they are creative explanations of how something got to be the way it is—for instance, how the monkey got his tail, how the giraffe got his long neck, or even how peanut brittle was invented. Some of the stories originated on cotton plantations, in lumber camps, or in oil fields. They were handed down from one person to another down through the ages. Some folk tales are written down, others are not. The ones we know about and hear the most often are those that have been written in books for children.

Reading folk tales to your class will get them interested in the simple beauty and marvelous adventures found in the stories. A few of the most appropriate folk tale books for classroom use are listed in the bibliography.

After the children have learned about folk tales and listened to them they will need no additional motivation to write them, just an invitation.

The following folk tale was written by a fifth grade girl.

How the Pencil Was Invented

One day when workers were bringing lead out of the mountains a great big man walked up. He must have been two hundred feet high! He said to the boss, "Do you have a job open?" The boss looked him over (from a ladder) and said, "What's your name?" And the man said, "Little Biddy Big John." Then the boss said, "It figgers." Then Little Biddy Big John said, "How about that job?" The boss said, "Sure. Big Bad John you show him where to work." Big Bad John said, "OK."

Then Big Bad John said to Little Biddy Big John, "You'll work here. Now get to work!" So Little Biddy Big John said, "Yes sir!" He didn't like Big Bad John very much. Then one day Little Biddy Big John pulled out a great big piece of lead. He accidentally dropped it and it went down the middle of a tree. Then Little Biddy Big John pulled up the tree. Then he said, "Boy oh boy, this sure makes a good pencil!" All the men cheered and said, "You found the best pencil ever known. When we write we won't get our hands dirty!" So from that day on they made pencils like that except they aren't 150 feet high. We should all thank Little Biddy Big John for discovering pencils.

Story Writing as an Enrichment Activity

Your regular social studies, science, and music units provide obvious opportunities for story writing. In science while you are studying the planets, for example, the class may want to write stories about life on another planet. If they are studying rocks or shells they might want to write about a fictitious new discovery made at the seashore or in the mountains.

One activity that children in the primary grades enjoy is composing "piano stories." You, as their leader, can start a story about a runaway goblin, a bear in a forest, a big giant, and so on. Pick subjects that would have definite high, low, heavy, or light sounds. That is, a giant's steps would be hard and low, a runaway goblin would sound high and fast. As you begin the story, accompany yourself with sound effects on the piano. Then let a child continue the story and try his own sound effects with the piano or simple rhythm instruments. If the story is a particularly interesting and pleasing one you could record it on chart paper as a cooperative class activity and use it again and again.

In one third grade class that I taught we were studying the Pueblo Indians for Social Studies. In the course of our reading about the Indians we came across several Indian tales. Then some of the members of the class tried their hand at writing an Indian tale. The following is the beginning of an Indian tale written by a third grade girl.

The Sun Carrier

The day that the Sun Carrier was born his parents were delighted. He was not a plain baby but was a gift from the great Sun himself. His parents named him Sun Carrier because around his middle a yellow line was there which he carried. There was almost a round circle with points on the end that was around his head. He grew into a fine and strong boy. He helped his father throw the sunbeams. Once he stumbled and spilled the sunbeams. He tried to pick them up but they stuck to the sky.

In a fifth grade class we were studying the explorers. One day the children tried writing a fictitious page in the diary of Leif Ericson using factual material they had acquired from their Social

Studies books as background. The following are some samples of the diary entries.

> I would not let the men go on the land we found right away because I was afraid that there may be enemies on it. Then I waited until a day later. I let some of the men go on but I told them to carry spears and shields. I told the rest of the men to stay down near the boat. Thyrker and I climbed a rocky cliff.

> It has been almost one month now. Our food and water are running low. We should have been in Greenland two days ago. The men are getting restless. The wind must have blown us off our course. The men are asleep now and I am the only one up. It has been an hour now and I do not see any sign of land.

> We have just landed in a far-off land. We will explore it tomorrow. We do not know what kind of people are on this land or even if there are any people here. We are going to stay aboard ship tonight, since we do not know anything about this strange land.

After the children have had experience at something like this you could mention the fact that they have written in the first person. It is not necessary that they know it, but it is an easy term for them to understand and may be helpful later if you want them to do something similar.

Let Storybook Characters Help

A favorite storybook may have just the motivation you need for your next creative writing lesson. You could have a book in which the characters are so real and so much fun to hear about that your class would want to use the characters as their own and put them in new stories and in new situations.

One fifth grade group responded with great enthusiasm to listening to a chapter from *Pinocchio* every day and it became evident that the class was going to be very disappointed when I reached the end of the book and they could no longer envision themselves in Pinocchio's world. Consequently, we decided that

Pinocchio would be able to do even more things and get involved in many more escapades if each one in the room would write another chapter in Pinocchio's life.

No restrictions were placed on things that could happen to him and no specific length requirements were made. The only suggestions given to the writer were that the events should be totally original and, if possible, the characters, with the exception of Pinocchio, should all be new ones.

Each child came up with some sort of a "chapter." The new ideas they created and the original use of dialogue were particularly intriguing to them when we read the stories back to the class.

On the following pages are some short portions from their chapters.

> Pinocchio had been wandering in the Woods of Wonders for some time now. By now he had met the Glowrabbit, the Bumblebear, and the Bald HairHare. These and other friends warned him to beware of the mad Dinglefrangle. All of the animals feared him. He was the only mean animal in the woods.
>
> One day Pinocchio was walking in the woods when he heard a loud, distant roar. Suddenly many animals came rushing away from the sound. Some were screaming and some were shouting, "Run from the Dinglefrangle!"
>
> Pinoccho just stood there like a statue. Then it came! The mad Dinglefrangle was bigger than anything he had ever seen in his whole life.
>
> It had the body of a person, the head of a fish, a bear, a person and a fox combined. He was as tall as a six story building, and was a sickly color of green.
>
> As soon as he saw Pinocchio, the mad Dinglefrangle grabbed him with a dirty green hand and took him to his cave.
>
> In the cave Pinocchio was put in a dirty, wet, bloody cage. There was an empty spit in a fire by the cage. Pinocchio decided not to let the mad Dinglefrangle cook him. So, in the middle of the night, Pinocchio worked at the bars. Evidently the bars had been worked on before, because they were weak and worn.
>
> Pinocchio finally got out and began to search the cave. He managed to find an old sword. It was heavy and sharp.

* * *

One day Pinocchio decided he would fly. First he watched a bird and he said, "All I have to do is flap my arms." So he got up on a roof. It wasn't a very big house. When he jumped off he landed right in a stand full of peaches. You can imagine what happened, "Splat," right into the stand. The people were so mad they ran him out of town.

* * *

One day when Pinocchio was in school his teacher said, "Pinocchio, what in tarnation are you doing?"

"I'm doing my Arithmetic, as usual," said Pinocchio.

"Are you copying off Julie's paper?"

"No," said Pinocchio in a shouting voice.

"Julie and Pinocchio bring your Arithmetic papers to me," said the teacher.

As she was examining the papers to see if they were alike the word LIAR appeared on Pinocchio's face. Feeling the word appearing, his face turned red. Then to himself he said, "Oh, oh no! Now what? How can I ever get rid of this word?"

I know!!! I'll pretend I have a headache and I'll hold my whole head so that Miss Snickleworth, my teacher, won't see the word.

* * *

One day when Pinocchio was walking home he met a devil.

"Why—What are you doing here?" he asked.

"Waiting for you," answered the devil.

"What do you want with me?"

"I want to take you to the Land of Bad Boys and Marionettes," he answered.

Pinocchio thought to himself, I love my mother and I dont want to leave her. Faster than you can say winka-do, (which is very fast), he was off and running.

* * *

One day Pinocchio was walking through the meadow when a woodpecker landed on his shoulder. The woodpecker started pecking at it. Pinocchio was very frightened for he knew what would happen if he didn't stop the woodpecker. Pinocchio would turn into a pile of sawdust. Then Pinocchio yelled, "Stop, stop!"

The woodpecker stopped and replied, "My son, what are you made of? You are mighty tasty." Then Pinocchio asked very politely after the woodpecker stopped, "What's your name and why do you want to eat me?" The woodpecker answered, "My name is Peskey Pest and I am very hungry."

"Well, that is no reason to eat me!" cried Pinocchio. "For there are other things to eat besides me."

"Yes, but you are the tastiest of all things," said Peskey.

Another book that I have found to be most delightful and adaptable for this type of creative writing is A. A. Milne's *Winnie the Pooh*. The lovable figures of Pooh Bear and his friends can be put to use quite easily.

Those who are familiar with the animal playmates of Christopher Robin realize the humor inherent in their intriguing escapades. However, before using a book such as *Winnie the Pooh* the children should become thoroughly familiar with the characters.

This familiarity can be realized after a period of reading from one of Milne's books and then discussing what types of "persons" Piglet, Rabbit, Eeyore, Kanga, and the others might be. It is then that a bond will grow between the listeners and the fictional characters. After you sense a rapport between the audience and the author you can begin to motivate the children to use the characters in their own stories. "Which character would you like best to have for your friend?" "What would you do if Pooh Bear came to your house?" "How would you like to take all of Milne's characters on a trip?" You and the class can discuss these questions. Then they will be ready to take the characters, with whom they are already acquainted, and provide them with new backgrounds and new situations.

Dictated Stories

In the primary grades, much use is being made of the dictation technique. The child simply creates the story in his mind and then dictates it to the teacher. After an initial discussion of what type of story he is going to think about (if it is to be a specific type), the child tells the story to the teacher, who writes or types it.

An effective technique with small children when they are telling their stories is to use a primary typewriter so they can watch their stories being written and can see the words appear before their eyes as they say them. This, incidentally, is often a very effective way of enlarging a child's reading ability. If he does much dictating he will soon recognize words from his speaking vocabulary that he previously did not know how to read or spell.

In this type of writing, a child's story will usually be more lengthy and the words he uses more difficult, since he does not have to struggle with writing them down or using the proper spelling.

Following are two sample stories dictated by second grade children. In the first story I doubt that the words *valuables* and *prehistoric* would have been used if the child had been writing the story down himself. Thus, it is a small example of the improved vocabulary resulting from dictation.

Watch Your Steps

I was walking in the woods one time and it started getting dark. I started to run and ran off a cliff. I went down, down, down.

"Plop."

There was a cave to the left side of me. I followed the cave and came to a room. It was filled with treasures—gold, famous pictures and valuables. I followed the cave and it led to another room. It was filled with prehistoric bones. I followed the cave and it led to stairs. I looked up the stairs and there was a little bit of light up there. I followed the stairs up and up and up.

Suddenly the light went out and I was back in my house in bed.

The Volcano Erupts

Once upon a time there was a giant volcano. Everybody thought it would erupt. A year later other people thought it wouldn't. The people who thought it would were right. It erupted. A giant eagle came out of it. It had been living in the volcano many years. It went around the world and took all the energy out of everybody. After it took the power from the people everything stopped working. No one had any energy to fight the bird.

Another volcano erupted. A gigantic bird bigger than the first one came out and killed the littler one. It gave all the energy back to the people. When the bird gave back the energy everything started to work and worked forever and the bird was their friend forever.

Although it is definitely easier for a child to dictate a story than it is for him to write it down, I would not ever use the dictation method exclusively. It has its advantages in that it is useful in beginning a creative writing program with the very young, in providing for a new outlet for older youngsters after they have done some writing on their own, or in encouraging and giving the nearly illiterate child a chance to create a story.

A Feeling of Freedom

You must remember that not every child will be in the mood to write the type of creative story you may have chosen to do on a particular day. Each time you have a creative writing period make it clear that the child can write a story of his own choosing. It does not have to be a story motivated by a title, a beginning read by the teacher, a picture, a character, a folk tale, an Indian tale, or a science lesson.

It just may happen that half of your class have some ideas of their own that they are anxious to get started on. This is wonderful. It is what you are aiming for in all the directed creative writing. It would be ideal if each time you had creative writing in your classroom each child already had his own creative ideas to work with. For that would mean that each child had truly been encouraged, motivated, and given the sense of security he needed in order to produce on his own.

The two following stories were turned in at the end of a creative writing period when the children had been given the choice of writing what they wished or writing one of the types of stories discussed previously.

The first story was written by a third grade girl without specific motivation.

The Bird Family

Hi. I'm a blue bird. I can fly in the sky. I can lay eggs. My eggs hatch into baby birds and the baby birds grow into big birds like me. My bluebirds can fly past the hills, past the clouds, and past the trees in the sky.

The Little Green Men from Squeaksville

Once upon a time there was a town on Mars. The town was called Squeaksville. The people who lived there were funny little green men who were called Squeaksvillians. They wanted to rule the whole universe so they planned to attack Earth.

These little men could change into flies so a scout came down to Earth in the form of a fly. A man was reading a newspaper and the fly kept buzzing around him and made the man angry so he got some BUG KILLER and sprayed it. It killed the fly. Therefore all the little men thought the Earthlings were too strong for them. Then they called off their plan of attack.

(Fifth grade boy)

The following story was written by a fourth grade girl. She supplied her own motivation—a dream.

The Hippopotamus

I was over at my grandmother's and it was a stormy night. It had been raining and had been very windy for a week. On the next day my grandmother had to go down the old jiggly stairs to do the wash that had been around for a week. She went down and was chased up by a hippopotamus. It was big and fat and had a tremendously huge mouth. She was almost dying to go to the store because we didn't have any food left. So she got a ride from a neighbor. She left me all alone in the spooky old house all by myself. I went down the jiggly stairs to give the hippopotamus some bread. It kept on backing up so I had to step into the flooded basement, flooded with rain water. When the water got deeper the hippopotamus just gobbled me up. Just like that as quick as a blink of your eye, and then I woke up from my dream.

Sometimes when you least expect it you may get a sudden splurge of creativity from a child who has let his own imagination lead him to write a polished gem. The poem that follows I found delightful, yet I did not ask for any poetry the day this was written.

The Lion Who Never Roared

Once there was a lion that would not roar,
He thought it was cowardly, too.
Soon he grew to be quite a bore
And he wouldn't make a noise, not even a moo!

The reason this lion would not make a sound
Was because he truly thought he would shake the ground.
One day he tried it and never again,
For this cowardly lion made a noise like a hen!

The Follow Up

After your class has begun to produce stories rapidly you may ask yourself, "What do I do with them?" If the stories need a lot of improving to be "good" how do you go about getting the improvement without discouraging the child? To begin with, stay away from your red pencil and your grammar handbook! Perfection is not important. What *is* important is the fact that you have encouraged your pupils to the point where they feel like being creative. That is the biggest and most important step.

Select what you feel to be the most promising thing in the story. It may be a character, the main theme, the setting, the dialogue, or the description. Comment heavily and favorably on that. Then you can approach the area that needs improvement almost matter-of-factly. "Your characters are excellent. I like Grandpa Drake. Could you find a way to put him in the middle of a little more action?" Or, "I could see the location of your story very clearly in my mind. It would make the story even more enjoyable if you could bring in a little more description."

The biggest danger in children's stories is the failure to have one important main event, or climax. Sometimes the child may even fail to have a theme (or "reason behind his story," to put it in the child's language). If you think the child could handle improvements, you could make suggestions to him. Many times the child will tend to clutter his story with so many happenings that the important things lose their impact and cause the reader to lose interest. In this case you can ask, "Which thing that happened in your story was the most important?" Then point out that he has not made this clear, that other things are taking away from the high point of the story. In a beginner's first or second try I would accept the story "as is" with no comments because getting the child to express his ideas without being self-conscious is more important than the technical details of a story.

After a child has experienced the fun of writing and is enjoying the creative process you can guide him with comments such as, "This is an excellent beginning. Can you think of a dramatic way to end it?" Or, "Your characters are very interesting and fun to read about but it is not always clear by their conversation which one is speaking. Can you make it more clear to the reader?"

The content and feel of conversation in stories are usually done well by children. They do not seem to be as overly conscious—as adult writers sometimes are—of the hazards of creating dialogue. When they write dialogue, it has an authentic ring to it, but it is often put down on paper just as if the reader should already know who is speaking. If this is the case with any of your pupils, you can discuss different ways to identify who is talking in the story. "Sally shouted," "Ben grumbled," "Jacqueline inquired," "Frank moaned," "the man shrieked," are the kinds of responses the children will come up with. They will have fun thinking of as many ways as possible to have people in their stories say things.

Directing the child's attention to the main theme, the dialogue, the description, and characters is quite enough in the elementary grades. If they are aware of these various elements in their stories and work on them they will be successful enough in their writing.

To dwell on plot content, structure, exposition, and the like, would be more discouraging to them than it would be helpful.

The teacher must keep in mind that all stories will not be suitable to read aloud but that the creation of them may nonetheless be important because it helps the child release some of his dreams and ideas. The finished product does not have to be of a high standard or even average. If it is an outlet for a child who needs it, it is a success.

4 *Writing Poetry*

We must remember that poetry means something a little different to each person. Each person is an individual in what he appreciates, enjoys hearing, and thinks is beautiful. What arouses *thought* and *emotion* in one person may not in another.

Just as no two faces are alike, nor two thumbprints alike, neither are any two personalities the same. Each person will think and interpret things in his own way. Thus, people evaluate poems in terms of their own appreciation, their own needs, and their own experiences.

In the past, poetry has suffered many abuses in the classroom. In some cases it has been used as an assignment, where the pupil had to memorize stanza after stanza to recite aloud. In other cases it has been read only on special occasions and only when relevant to a timely event, such as a cherry tree poem on George Washington's birthday or an Easter bunny poem before Easter. In some classrooms poetry has been read with vigor, but the teacher has selected poems that go *da, dee, da, da da, dee, da, da*. These are read in a sing-song voice and invariably end with a cute little twist. This kind of poetry background is one that present-day teachers must endeavor to change.

Poetry is an enormously exciting area to explore with a group of children. Very small children often have a natural appreciation and knack for poetry. They speak it, they see it, they delight in it. For example, "Sister melted, Francine came out," is the way one four-year-old expressed the change in his sister's personality.

Children are sensitive to changes of emotion and are almost hypersensitive in picking up and reflecting the emotions of others. Because of this they are innate poets. *The teacher's challenge is to release the poetry that is waiting within their minds and hearts.*

To erase the stereotyped conceptions that children have about what poetry is and what it sounds like, the teacher should first build a selective poetry file. Poems that will reap the best "writing harvest" from the youngsters in the long run are the ones that *do not rhyme* but do one or more of the following things:

1. Appeal quite strongly to the senses.
2. Have subject matter that relates to something a child may have experienced.
3. Have a vocabulary that is not too much beyond the reading vocabulary of the age group.
4. Express genuine emotion.
5. Provoke a mental picture in the reader's mind.
6. Express an appealing or thought-provoking idea.

Free verse will usually do several of these things. You will find that children's poems that do not have specific rhyme patterns will usually have more in the way of thought content and more concentration on beauty or emotion. They will not be entertaining just for entertainment's sake, or clever for the sake of cleverness, but they will be something more—something closer to the heart of the child.

The Poetry File

I have mentioned the use of a poetry file. The best way to keep a workable and handy poetry file to use in the classroom is to type or print your selected poems on 3 x 5 cards with the poem on the front and the source on the back. I have one poetry file of carefully selected free verse which I read to the children periodically to give them a background of poetry, for appreciation's sake.

I keep another file of free verse written by children—poems that I think would inspire other children to write. I use these poems as incentives immediately before the class begins a poetry writing session.

Once you have a basic file with several poems for your grade level, you will have a starting point for many hours of poetry appreciation in your classroom, hours you can spend reading, discussing, and interpreting poetry.

Getting in the Mood

It is best to start out by using only two or three poems, reading them at a certain time each day when you feel the class is relaxed—such as the first thing in the morning or before Reading, but not after Physical Education or immediately before lunch when the children's minds are restless and their bodies are not relaxed.

Sometimes the pupils may enjoy closing their eyes and listening to a descriptive poem and then telling what they pictured in their minds. We will say more about mental pictures later, but the technique is basically the same for guiding the class in poetry as it is for description. Let them tell how a poem makes them use their senses—what the poetry makes them see, hear, taste, feel, and smell.

More and more free verse is being written for children but it is still not an easy job to find poems that serve as good examples for classroom poetry appreciation.

I have included in this chapter a starter group of poems for children which are thorough in their attempts at producing emotions and are pure in their quality without being contrived. With each poem is a note on how to use it in the classroom.

What I Like Most

What I like most
   is for my friend and I
to have the same thought
   at the same moment.

What I like most
   is helping something
wonderful happen
   by just being me.

What I like most
   is holding
my little sister's hand
   when she is walking
to make her feel safe.

Most of the time
   it's what I like most
that counts.

"What I Like Most" is an easy poem to read and use in the primary grades. All the children can react to it because each one will have something that he likes most. After reading the poem through a couple of times, ask the children what they can add to it. Their suggestions can be listed on large sheets of chart paper in front of the class. When they have finished, the most original or the most poetic suggestions can be selected from the list and put together to form a cooperative class poem.

Old Friends

A tiny chair too small for me
to sit in anymore
A stuffed toy dog with spots,
threadbare
Some roller skates I had
when I was four . . .

All those things
that I don't play with
now that I'm too big for them
are kept in a very, secret
closet place
away from everything that's new.

There they sit, like old friends
that I like to visit now and then
as I grow up.

"Old Friends" brings up another universal topic among younger children. All of them will have old toys of which they are particularly fond. After reading the poem to the children, ask them what kinds of old toys or playthings they have. Where are they kept? What do they look like? What do they think the author meant by "a very, secret closet place"? How would the inside of a closet look? Would it be dark and old? Would it be big enough for them to walk inside and sit down?

Each child might like to write one sentence about one favorite old toy and draw a picture to go with it. These could be collected in a booklet for the whole class to enjoy.

In My Dreams

I saw a marshmallow creme horse
in my dream. And I ate it.

I saw a green ice-cream sky
in my dream. And I licked it.

I saw a rose spun of gold and silver
in my dream. And I held it.

I saw a desert camel all beautifully decked
in my dream. And I rode it
. . . until I reached reality again.

After reading "In My Dreams" to little children, I would discuss with them the meaning of the word *reality*. Talk about what is real and what is not real in order for them to develop a clear understanding of the word. Then read the poem again and have them listen for the unreal things. See if they can describe them. Ask them about their dreams. What things do they see? There will undoubtedly be a lot of invention on the part of the children, in order to answer the question, so they will definitely be performing creatively. This poem serves as a good stimulus for the writing of one-line poems in the first or second grade. Each child can write about and describe, as clearly as possible, something he has seen in a dream or something he would *like* to see. The poem acts, specifically, as a motivating force to set their imaginations free.

Silly Words

Like a juggler juggling oranges
I can throw words in the air
And jiggle them, and joggle them
Until their letters get all jumbled up.
The words come out muddled-mixed
And I talk to my friends with them
In a secret, silly language
That grown-ups don't understand.

This little poem can be used to develop a very interesting discussion of what is meant by "silly words." The children can talk about various words that might be juggled around until the sounds are different. They might try to talk in their own "secret language."

Have the children suggest how they feel about other kinds of words, like "scolding words" or "nice words," or "words that make you feel good."

The Actress

Night is
a tall thin lady
trailing across the sky
in a black-veiled skirt
whispering and whishing
like a creature who never sleeps
but walks proudly with her dress
trailing behind her
until . . . bold sun
sends her skim, skimming away
to wait somewhere
for her next appearance.

Night Robber

Night comes with a cool, black mask
to cover the face of daylight
and the only lights that you can see
are the night-robbers' eyes
glistening like stars
through the holes in his mask.

Morning

Day creeps onto me with warmness
and inches yellow light along my skin
as I lie in my bed in morning
under my quilt that is the color of sun.

The Sky Has Cooked the Sun Today

The sky has cooked the sun today
and I watch it sizzle
fried around the edges to a golden yellow
glowing in the sky-blue pan
that fills the space above my head.

After reading the two night poems, "The Actress" and "Night Robber," read the two poems about day, "Morning" and "The Sky Has Cooked the Sun Today." Ask the children to compare the differences in imagery. Specifically point out the comparisons in lines such as "Night comes with a cool, black mask / to cover the face of daylight" and "Day creeps onto me with warmness." Talk about "The Actress." Who is she? Describe how she looks. Is she brave or timid? What does *bold* sun mean? What other words can we use to describe the sun as a person?

When talking about "The Sky Has Cooked the Sun Today," have the children describe what kind of a day it is in the poem. Is it a winter or summer day? Where do you suppose the poet was? Then see if the children can develop, orally, their own original ways of telling about night coming or day breaking. Ask how many have ever seen the sun rise? What was its color? Did it seem close or far away? Did it give off any heat? What colors were in the sky? Was it a quiet or noisy time of day?

Old Man

For some reason I cannot explain
that old man was fascinating
for me to see

hobbling, so much wiser
than I
down the street
with his hunched hand
on the top of his cane.

Read this through twice and ask the children questions to stimu-late their imaginations in respect to developing the man more fully as a character. What did he have on? How old do you think he was? What would give you an idea about his age? Why did the poet feel that he was wise? Ask them if they have ever been fascinated by someone they saw but did not know. Let them tell about it.

The World Today

I saw the world today
through red balloons
bobbing in front of me
at the zoo

causing even the giraffes
to prance around in pink.

In just a few words, "The World Today" gives the reader a clear, perceptive vision of what the poet sees. Have the children try, with a few words, to describe some vision in a similar way using subjects such as what the sea looks like when you are under its surface, the view of the ground from an airplane, or the back yard from a tree top.

Seventy and Seven Silver Charms

Seventy and seven silver charms for sale
are carried on the arms of the tall Senora
who strides through the streets of Mexico
selling silver and glittering in the sun
like a proud bird with metallic wings.

For more advanced groups, this poem offers a good example of alliteration, which is the repetition of initial consonants that serve to unify the poem. In this case the repetition of *s* sounds is effective in unifying the poem. Have the children listen to the alliteration in the "Seventy and seven silver charms for sale" and, "Senora / who strides through the streets of Mexico / selling silver and glittering in the sun."

This poem would also serve as a lovely incentive for an art lesson. Have the children put down their visual impressions of the senora. They can use a variety of media—water colors, poster paint, chalk, tissue paper, clay, mosaics, and so forth. In the comparisons of their pictures they will be able to see how the *same* poem created *different* mental images.

Jazz

Like something moving
  in a shadowed room
    the jazz came
      slow
        and cool
billowing, blowing
        my pinwheel heart
round and round
       with its sound
crashing and blasting
      and splin
          ter shattering
then moaning off to a thin wail
         before it stopped.
And its instruments
     leaned
       against
        the
         wall
          to gasp for breath.

"Jazz" is the kind of poem that appeals to upper grade children. The form in which it is written is fun for them to *see*. When it is presented it can be written on the chalkboard, a piece of chart paper, or it could be flashed on a screen from an overhead projector.

"Passing Stranger" should be read through several times before beginning a discussion of it. Like "Jazz," it is a good poem for the children to see as well as hear, since its subject matter dictates its form. It is written to give the reader the feeling of the man being seen from a distance at first and then approaching until he is at close range.

Discussion of the last six lines can be quite thought-provoking. They are particularly conducive to motivating individual interpretation. The children will have to "fill in" meanings, to delve further into the poet's intent, to draw their own conclusions about the poem. What do the lines, "and I knew his eyes had seen / their own seasons" mean? What kind of a life do you suppose the old man had? What occupation did he have? What does "his heart / had known its dignity" mean? How can a heart hold dignity? What kinds of things make a person proud? When the poet says "and his mouth / had many stories to tell" what did he have in mind? What kinds of stories do you think they could be? Would the word "stories" in the poem necessarily mean the kind of story we are familiar with? Could the word *experiences* be exchanged for *stories?*

Passing Stranger

From far off down the street
the man looked

    like he was dressed in brown paper bags
    crumpled and torn

       but when he came nearer

       I could see the bags were clothes
       and the leather hide that was his face
       hid crevices of smiles and frowns

       one hand reached up

       and roughly smoothed his brown and silvered hair

       and I knew his eyes had seen
       their own seasons
       his heart
       had known its dignity
       and his mouth
       had many stories to tell.

If this poem were to be used to the fullest the children might enjoy writing a story from an old man's point of view, or just telling stories aloud as if they themselves were old people. It is a good poem for stimulating the imagination and motivating the children for role playing.

Forming Mental Pictures

I have used the term *mental pictures* several times. You may ask yourself, "Just what *is* a mental picture?" For example, the poem "Old Friends" mentions a tiny chair, a stuffed toy dog, and roller skates, but does not describe them in detail. However, the reader can draw his own pictures of these things. The class can describe aloud what the stuffed toy dog might look like. In other words, they can interpret for themselves what images the poem produces in their minds. This interpretation is made possible by the evidence the poet has given the reader, what he has already *told* the reader. Part of the mental picture will consist of what the poet has already supplied the reader with and part will be the reader's own interpretation according to what he wants to see and is capable of seeing. Different children may come up with very different mental pictures using the same line of poetry for a stimulus.

In "Seven and Seventy Silver Charms," each child may have a different picture of the senora in his mind. Some might see her as an old woman, some as a young woman, some as a fat woman with a serape. That is why I suggested an art lesson in conjunction with this particular poem. It is interesting for the children to compare their mental pictures with each other. This could be done with a great many of the poems listed in the file.

The Use of Music

Music is also an effective means of stimulating mental pictures in children's minds. Select a piece of music that is definitely dramatic in some way so that it will provoke thought and stimulate the imagination. It need not be loud or wild but it should definitely have enough variation in it to hold your young listeners' interest. Before playing the music tell the children that you want them to see what they can imagine while they are listening, something that would go with that kind of music. Do not mention the title of the selection you are going to play because then the children can be lazy and merely repeat what they think the title implies.

It is amazing how the children respond to music with mental pictures that are pure poetry in themselves.

Following are the responses a third grade class gave after listening to *Ritual Fire Dance.*

> chariots racing
> a garden full of bees and other insects going after their enemies
> some natives marching through a factory
> white horses running around in a ring at a circus with a lady on one
>   side
> girls dancing in Egypt

It is very enjoyable to do this exercise with a class. It takes little effort on their part but nevertheless is rewarding. After they have listened to the music and shared their mental pictures, you can tell them the name of the recording. They will enjoy comparing what they visualized with what the composer had in mind when he wrote the selection.

Following are some interesting examples obtained from a third grade class after listening to several different recordings:

Aviary

birds flying up in the sky

a butterfly flying fast up and down on a windy night

a little girl talking to a bird and talking bird sounds so the bird would
   understand her

an owl singing

a waterfall going down and bumping into rocks

swans swimming around in the water with the sun shining over

pixies coming out of a mushroom house and dancing

a butterfly on a cool summer morning passing flowers

Fossils

two mice creeping to the refrigerator and suddenly a cat coming over

a girl and boy tiptoeing in to see a new girl who moved in

an Indian sneaking up on a deer

elves playing music on lilies

a boy and girl on ice skates tiptoeing

baby birds just popping out of their shells . . . their mother is teaching
   them how to talk

Dance of the Buffoons

a clown

people doing things real fast

a magician doing tricks

tiny people in an old tree stump making music

horses trampling people

headhunters running after a man

Dance of the Sugar Plum Fairy

people sitting in an audience watching a play

German ballet dancers doing a recital dance

fairies waving wands

gypsies dancing around a fire

You will notice that the children came up with some mental
pictures they could use in writing poetry. In the images provoked
by *Aviary*, one of them in particular could well be the beginning
of a free verse poem:

> A butterfly flying fast
> up and down
> on a windy night

The child will probably not recognize these musically motivated mental pictures as good poetry material but after you have acted pleased and have encouraged him to add to it, he will realize that it is just this kind of imagination from which poetry comes.

As an experiment with a fifth grade class, I played two phonograph records. The first one was a fast Dixieland jazz selection and the second was a slow, brassy piece which changed midway to a mournful burial dirge. During each one I had the children jot down any words or mental pictures that came into their minds. After they had listened to the records they were free to develop a poem from the "notes" they had taken during the listening period.

Following are several poems written after listening to the Dixieland tune.

Oh, here comes the parade!
With the band and the music so gay
and its bright, shiney instruments.
One sounds like a bird twittering away
Another sounds like its way down in the blues.
And don't forget the players
Their suits are of the color red
And then behind the band comes the juggler
Juggling away.

* * *

The trombone is a funny thing
It sounds like a funny voice
If I wanted a funnier thing
A tuba'd be my choice

* * *

Today the sun in shining out in the clear, blue sky
I stand up by the window and hear the clapping of hands
And the action of instruments playing in the town.

The following poems were written after listening to the second selection, the funeral dirge that started with a fast tempo and gradually became slower.

It's too bad Jake had to go
but don't mourn too long
for the world is waiting
for a joyous song

Don't mourn over Jake
because he's dead and gone
and he won't mean much
to a happy world.

* * *

A long time ago in the south
when somebody died
a lot of people would line the street
on a dull day to cry.

When they were buried
people would stop crying
but they knew someday they would die
and people would cry then too.

* * *

The Civil War had started.
The cannons burst in fire.
Shots and bolts flew everywhere
The cannons roared with thunder
And then everything was in dead silence
And the stars shone no more
Everybody went to that happy place
Dixieland.

The serious tone of these poems shows that the children were able to capture the mood of the music and to let their imaginations go. I must confess that I was pleased with the depth shown in them. I would not use records of mournful quality often, but it is good to use something such as this once in a while for a change of pace and to give some variety to the class.

Writing Free Verse

I have talked much about free verse and have given many examples of free verse in the poetry file.

Free verse is *not* something new and strange that has been contrived by a new generation. It is a free form of poetic expression. It is poetry without definite structure, without rhyme, and without rules, so to speak. It is a form of poetry that existed long before the alphabet existed. It is the first type of poetry we ever had in our world—that spoken by one person to another.

There are things all around you that can be put to use in helping poetry grow in your classroom—for example, the weather, an experience you all have together, music, sounds from the outside, feelings of hunger, happiness, or tiredness. All these things can inspire the creation of poetry.

For example, using a small rhythm-band drum in the classroom can be inventive. The teacher can hit the drum, using several beats —heavy and hard beats, staccato beats, or a smooth brushing sound with the palm of the hand. Have the children listen and select words that will match the beats. Just as a small child will say, "A big man goes boom-boom on our house," to describe a heavy rainstorm, the children in the classroom could tell what the sounds remind them of and perhaps with this device write a cooperative poem.

The use of one isolated word to bring forth mental images is also an interesting way to stimulate mental pictures. In doing this the teacher or a child suggests a word that will bring some immediate mental picture. Words like *hit*, *slide*, *screech*, or *fright* will bring images to mind. Use this for a game type of activity—for enjoyment—and see how many different things the class can suggest, using one word as a stimulus.

For instance the word *slide* may call to mind these images:

A hot and dusty baseball player in a blue uniform sliding into first.

A fried egg sliding from one side of the plate to another as a person carries it to the table.

A small child whizzing down a slide in a park.

The children may like to bring in words that they think are particularly useful for provoking mental images and use them on the rest of the class. This is good creative mental exercise and helps develop a quick reflex to hearing or thinking words, which is helpful indeed in writing poetry.

Although free verse is a written form of poetry, it is also all around us in the spoken word. We have only to sharpen our sense of hearing and train ourselves to listen with sensitivity in order to hear it.

When we encourage children to write poetry or free verse, we are, in a sense, encouraging them to release that which is already within them. It is a matter of channeling it and of recording it.

After you have used a poetry file with a class and used music and other things to evoke poetic images, and after a few sessions of talking at ease with your class about things, places, and feelings they especially like or dislike, your students will begin to bring out and express definite ways of feeling which is what a poet must have before he can record his observations and reflections.

After the children have selected topics for their poems, encourage them not to be too critical of the way in which they record their feelings or their mental pictures. It is more important to record the images as they come and rearrange them later, if they need to. At all times the essential thing for the students to remember is to convey some feeling or idea, to worry little about *how* it is being expressed and more about *what* is being expressed. That is, if the poem seems to have too many words in one line, that is not as important as the thought or emotion expressed in that line.

The fifth grade girl who wrote "The Storm" could certainly have improved on the form of her poem if she had been forced to, but it was accepted as it was written with little change. The result is that this particular poem is extremely original and delightful in part, and writing it was a satisfying experience for the child.

The Storm

The storm is unfriendly.
It grumbles and groans
when it's mad.
It shouts bursts of lightening.
It's not a bit friendly
or kind to people.

It roars with thunder.

The following poem was written by a fifth grade boy who seemed unable to do his regular written work. It was only when the class started creative writing that he began to take an interest in anything. It was, in fact, the only area in which he could be justly praised. Even though the poem is not one of depth, it is definitely one of mood and the other children in the room were able to pick up the mood of this poem and appreciate it.

Oh, how I like to go camping out at night
with the flickering of firelight on my face
and trees surrounding me.
Suddenly I hear a voice out of the dark, dark night.
I wonder what it could be.
As a chill runs down my back suddenly I hear it again.
"Oh, don't be frightened,"
It's only an owl.

The following free verse was written after some reading of poetry and discussion of it. "Run" was one of the first efforts of a fifth grade girl.

Run

When I run
I think I'm a race horse.
I run with great speed.
Or like a bullet,
In flight to its destiny.
But just like a bullet
I have to stop sometime.

"Run" shows thought and sensitivity, the two things the creative writing teacher should aim at getting the children to use and demonstrate.

As with stories, the first-effort poems have to be praised, read aloud, shared with the group, displayed, and referred to in order for the child to think that what he has done is worthwhile and is something worth doing and trying to improve. *The attitude with which these first efforts are received will play an all-important part in the future creative productivity of a class.*

As I mentioned previously, children will enjoy hearing poems by other children—especially other children whom they know—more than they will hearing poetry written by adults. So by exposing your pupils to a beginning poetry file and to each other's efforts they will begin to be motivated more and more toward new ideas and new ways of expressing them.

Writing Haiku

Haiku is a form of Japanese poetry that usually centers around nature. The haiku is difficult to write in that the first line must have five syllables, the second line seven syllables, and the last line five syllables. The three lines together generally express a continuous thought.

Amazingly enough, children are not at all reluctant to try doing something as structured as haiku. In fact, they accept it as a challenge and have a good time with it. Because of their rigid

form, haiku take time and thought and, of course, an understanding of how to recognize syllables.

Fourth, fifth, and sixth grade classes and up should already be
familiar with the meaning of the word *syllable*. It is vital that the
children understand exactly what a syllable is before they try to
write haiku. If they are not sure how to determine the number of
syllables a word has then they will need to learn.

The easiest way to explain it is to help them discover that a
syllable is a part of a word that contains one vowel sound (not
just one vowel necessarily, but one vowel *sound*). Use words such
as *cake* or *street* to start with. There are two vowels in each of these
words but only one vowel sound in each, so each word has one
syllable. In the word *kindergarten* all the vowels can be heard. There
are four vowel sounds; therefore, there are four syllables.

Have the children practice recognizing syllables by saying their
own last names, listening for the vowel sounds, and then telling
how many syllables each person's last name has. As a general rule,
children will pick this concept up quite rapidly.

After discussing the structure of haiku with the children and
explaining to them that haiku usually deal with nature, they can
listen to some haiku with a more defining and appreciative ear. A
book of haiku from the library would be a good way to introduce
your class to the form.

There are many delightful haiku that can be used to inspire your
class. Some of the best are reprinted below.

> Melting snow waters
>   thrill down mountainsides, washing
> spring in, winter out.

> Brown hands place blossoms
>   in a bowl, then stand aside
> to admire their work.

> Rippling moon riding
>   on the sea mends, breaks, gathers
> together again.

The sun trickling through
    thick pine tree branches dots the
forest floor with light.

The following haiku were written by fifth grade students after
a few listening and discussing sessions.

The soft, mossy earth
    lies like a fuzzy brown bear
in the star-filled woods.

The cat lies waiting
    then springs and catches his prey
which was his shadow.

The boat moved slowly
    up the St. Louis River
to its destiny.

There is a pretty
    black bird in a colored nest
dissolving a worm.

The small, white flower
    is open most of the day,
like a small mushroom.

My cat is creeping
    about the dark, still bedrooms
like a big lion.

5 *Creative Writing Projects*

In order for a child to have a feeling of accomplishment about his writing it is sometimes necessary or desirable—at least for him —for his writing efforts to culminate with a project of some sort. Children seem to have a natural inclination toward projects and often begin doing them at home for their own amusement or even at school when they are not required. Putting together something permanent from what he has done will help give the child a feeling of satisfaction and perhaps encourage him to achieve more in the creative field.

There are numerous projects that a child can undertake in connection with his writing. These can be divided into two categories —individual projects and group projects. With any project, once it has been selected, the child should make a written commitment of some sort, such as an outline of the plot or a statement about the contents of his project. This will help him to clarify in his own mind what he is going to try to do and therefore more clearly define his objective for himself.

51

Long Stories

Working on an individual basis, a child may decide to write a story of a specific length, for example, a folk tale, mystery story, a fantasy, or an experience he has had, that will run 600 words or more.

In writing a story of this length the writer will need to do quite a bit of planning and should ask himself these questions before beginning:

1. Who are my readers going to be? Shall I aim my story at children my own age or younger?
2. Which of my characters will be my main character and from which character's viewpoint will I tell my story?
3. What is the main theme or main idea of the story?
4. What emotions will I make the reader feel?

These four questions are enough for an average child to deal with. Of course, there are numerous questions an author can ask himself but with elementary pupils or young teen-agers these guidelines should be sufficient. After the story is finished it can be bound in a cardboard folder, hand lettered and decorated, or it can be put in a cloth binding or something else that suits the writer's fancy.

Making Books

Some children may enjoy doing individual projects for younger children. A fifth or sixth grader will have fun writing and illustrating a book for a younger child. In this case he will have to keep in mind what would interest a younger child and what kind of vocabulary he should use.

In constructing a book for a younger child, the *text should be completed first and then the parts the writer wants to illustrate should be selected.* Otherwise, the child may become more involved in what he is drawing than in what he is writing.

A book of haiku with illustrations makes a nice gift for parents and is a way of combining two kinds of creative talent. Ten or twelve haiku can be bound together with some carefully done watercolors or designs of some other media such as charcoal, conté crayon, or pastels. In keeping with the oriental motif, these "books" can be punched, laced, and tied in the Japanese fashion. (There are many craft books for classroom use that explain these art methods fully.)

Wall Hangings

A wall hanging can be made as a gift for relatives or friends. Start with a large rectangular piece of heavy material such as an 18″ x 26″ or 18″ x 30″ (depending on the line length of the poem) piece of felt or heavy burlap. Wrap each end around a wood or plastic rod and sew or glue securely. Use cut-up curtain rods, knitting needles, or plain wooden rods for the ends. Attach colored string or yarn to one end for securing the hanging to the wall. Let the child select a poem that he thinks would be suitable for a wall hanging and have him cut out the letters for his words from a different kind of material and then glue or sew them on.

A TV Show

To present a mock television show for other classes or parents, the class can select a story that someone in the room has written and divide it into parts. The parts can be read or acted out by different members of the class group. A narrator can be used to provide continuity to the performance. The children will enjoy making small props to use, arranging for sound effects, and developing their own entertaining commercials. A project such as this involves the participation of as many class members as is desirable and gives room for a lot of elaboration. Thus, it can be as simple or as complicated as the teacher or class wishes it to be.

Another type of television show would require the making of a TV box. A large, square cardboard box with a window cut in it will do. The box can be painted and knobs attached to it to make it resemble a television set. The knobs can be made from cardbox, wood, bottle caps, or the like. The story to be presented can be written in sections on a large, white paper scroll. Each written section can be followed by an illustration so that there will be one written part, one picture, another written part, another picture, and so on. The scroll can then be fastened inside the box and attached to a roller on the other side so that it can be wound from one side of the television box to the other as the audience views the show.

A Radio Program

Several members of the class may want to combine their stories to make a radio program to present to another class during their language arts period. This can be done easily. Each member should practice reading his story until he can read it with ease and expression. An announcer can give the name of each writer, who will then read his story. About five children with average-length stories will make a 15 or 20 minute radio program. The program can be presented "live," or it can be tape recorded.

Poetry Drawing Books

A poetry drawing book is another very good group project and one that can involve everyone in the room. Each child selects his best poem and letters it on a piece of white paper. These poems can be pasted on every other page in a tagboard loose-leaf booklet. The child's name and age can be written underneath his poem. On blank pages that are opposite the poems, the child can paste a piece of drawing paper. The child who receives the book can read the poems and then illustrate them as he sees fit on the blank pages. This project makes a wonderful gift for a hospitalized youngster.

A colorful potato-print design or wood-block design makes an attractive cover.

Story Calendars

Another interesting gift is a story calendar. From their stories the children of a class can select one story that seems particularly appropriate for each month. For instance, in March they may have *A Story Especially for March—Franz and His Flyaway Kite*. Twelve representative stories can be typed on dittoes and run off on a duplicating machine so that there will be a copy of each story for each child in the room. Starting with the January story, the stories can be stapled in consecutive order on the top half of a large piece of oak tag. Under the stories the calendar for that month can be glued or stapled. As each month passes, the story for the month will change along with the calendar. This project is especially fun for families with young children.

Grading the Projects

I have emphasized before that grading should be played down in creative work since it is the content we are interested in and the effect that the production of the creative writing has on the young writer. However, most teachers feel that it is necessary, especially for projects, to evaluate the student's work by giving it some sort of grade. I have always followed a dual grading system in marking projects. First, the child is graded for the original ideas, interest, and completeness of his creative work. Second, he is given a grade that I call a mechanical grade because it evaluates his spelling, punctuation, neatness, and the actual construction of his project. Both grades have equal value but I feel that it is important for a child to know that even though he may have erred in constructing his wall hanging, or been ineffective in reading his story for a radio program, that the poem or the story itself was good and had creative merit.

6 *Maintaining the Creative Climate*

Once begun, creativity in the classroom can become a giant snowball rolling and gathering momentum as it goes. Successful creativity produces feelings of self-confidence, accomplishment, and satisfaction in the teacher; but since the teacher is the mainstay in the processes of motivation, inspiration, and encouragement, it is up to him to *maintain* the creative climate, to keep it alive and to keep it producing.

After a while you may find yourself saying, "I'm glad they're writing but what shall I do when it slows down?" First of all, it *will* slow down. It is only natural that children—and adults too, for that matter—will have a period in which to reflect, in which to appreciate the creativity of others and let their own rest. It is impossible for anyone to sustain a constant mood of productiveness in anything without some diversion. So when this occurs and one of your prize writers begins to slow down, let him be. After a period of time, with your help, his talent will spark again.

The Incubation Period

There is a period in which ideas begin to formulate, in which ordinary things take on new meanings, in which common everyday sights take on new appearances. At this time the child or adult, as the case may be, acquires a renewed enthusiasm for what he is doing and he longs to get started expressing himself. I call this the incubation period, the period in which things start to grow, to sprout, and to take hold.

Time and patience are needed on your part in helping someone who has an idea he wants to develop into a story or poem but does not know how to go about it. For instance, a child may say, "I want to write a mystery story about our camping trip." You, as a teacher, know that a mystery story is very difficult to write. Do not discourage your young aspirant. You might suggest to him, "Write down the ideas you have for your story and then list the characters you are going to use." After he had done that he may be at a loss to know what to do next with the story he wants to tell. Again you could suggest, "Write down the things that will happen in your story one by one. Underline the things you think are most important." Your next step would be to suggest an outline of the main ideas and events that the child has listed. In other words, you are the guiding hand and are helping the child to write down what is trying to organize itself in his mind.

Awareness of the Child's Perception

As I mentioned before, it is actually a game to try and help children be more perceptive. In my own experiences I have found that the youngest children usually beat me at my own game.

That is to say, they are often more perceptive about physical things in the world than I am, probably because they are less used to seeing things around them. Also, they are less inhibited about voicing their discoveries.

Recently a five-year-old brightened my morning when I walked out of my house to get into my car and was dismayed by the drizzling, gray weather. "When it rains," she said in a tiny, quizzical voice, "I wonder why it doesn't make holes in the sky."

Respecting Nonconformity

In our present-day world of rebellion, we have developed a certain way of thinking about nonconformity as being a stereo-typed position of defiance. It is not. At least the kind of non-conformity I am referring to is not. To respect an idea that does not fit into the pattern of what we want the class to think is sometimes hard to do. We have certain ways of arriving at answers and we have been conditioned to approach things in certain ways. Often we are not at all content when someone else has a different approach or viewpoint, especially if it does not coincide with our teaching aims.

A child who consistently has different ways of interpreting meanings or who is always in the minority because of his opinions, may, quite often, have something to say that is valuable. It may be an idea for your whole group to listen to, discuss, and weigh in terms of its possible worth. Children who dream in class when they are supposed to be working will often be the ones with differing views. Listen to what they have to say. It may be surprisingly original and interesting.

Flexibility in the Curriculum

It is vital in a creative environment to have sufficient flexibility to allow the teacher to enlarge upon a creative opportunity whenever one presents itself. This cannot *always* be done, but many times it can be. If, during a spelling lesson, for example, someone uses a word in a particularly poetic way, call attention to it, enlarge upon it. If, during the reading period, a child is particularly delighted with a story and shows his enjoyment, give him the opportunity to use the same characters from the story in his own story or play. If, in the primary grades, a child brings in something for sharing that has artistic value—a picture, a flower, or the like—let the children describe it together. See how many different descriptive words they can gather together to describe the object.

If, now and then, little original spurts of enthusiasm are allowed to come creeping into the curriculum the classroom will be a more enjoyable and more challenging place for the teacher and the pupils alike.

A Guideline

Remember that to kindle creativity, *reading* is just as important as writing. *Hearing* is just as important as talking. *Seeing* is just as important as hearing about. Exposure to literature and poetry is half the creative process. Your reaction, encouragement, sympathy, and sensitivity make up the other half.